Apple Trees

by Dorothy Hinshaw Patent
photographs by William Muñoz

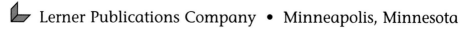

Lerner Publications Company • Minneapolis, Minnesota

For all the teachers who deserve a tasty apple each day!

The author and photographer want to thank Snokist Growers, Brad Tukey, Dick Zimmer, Art and Nancy Callan, and Albert and Wilma Park for their help with this book, with special thanks to Diane Bilderback for her comments on the manuscript.

Thanks to our series consultant, Sharyn Fenwick, elementary science/math specialist. Mrs. Fenwick was the winner of the National Science Teachers Association 1991 Distinguished Teaching Award. She also was the recipient of the Presidential Award for Excellence in Math and Science Teaching, representing the state of Minnesota at the elementary level in 1992.

Illustrations on pp. 10, 21, 25, and 38 by Laura Westlund, © Lerner Publications Company.

Early Bird Nature Books were conceptualized by Ruth Berman and designed by Steve Foley. Series editor is Joelle Goldman.

Library of Congress Cataloging-in-Publication Data

Patent, Dorothy Hinshaw.
    Apple Trees / by Dorothy Hinshaw Patent ; photographs by William Muñoz.
      p.   cm. — (Early bird nature books)
    Includes index.
      Summary: Describes the life cycle of an apple tree and how different varieties of apples are grown and harvested.
      ISBN 0-8225-3020-1 (alk. paper)
      1. Apples—Juvenile literature. 2. Apples—Life cycles—Juvenile literature. [1. Apples.] I. Muñoz, William. II. Title. III. Series.
    SB363.P35   1997
    634'.11—dc20   96-27581

Manufactured in the United States of America
1 2 3 4 5 6 – SP – 02 01 00 99 98 97

Contents

Be a Word Detective

Can you find these words as you read about the apple tree's life? Be a detective and try to figure out what they mean. You can turn to the glossary on page 46 for help.

auxin	nectar	rootstock
bud	ovary	seedling
carbon dioxide	petals	spurs
chlorophyll	pollen	stamens
grafting	pollinated	styles

Chapter 1

More apples are grown in the United States than in any other country. What kind of weather do apple trees need?

Our Favorite Fruit

Apples are the world's favorite fruit. People have been eating them for thousands of years. The first apple trees grew in Asia and Europe. When settlers first came to America, they carried apples with them. Apple trees grew well in their new home.

Apple trees grow best in places with cold winter weather. But they need warm summers, too. Apple trees grow well in much of the United States. They also grow in many other countries.

Wild apple trees grow in many parts of the world.

Chapter 2

This tree is loaded with many bright red apples. What fruits are relatives of the apple?

Big Trees and Little Ones

 Apples are relatives of strawberries, blackberries, and pears. Strawberries grow on

small plants. Blackberries grow on vines. But apples and pears grow on trees.

Apple trees grow from seeds. The seed has a hard coat. The hard coat protects the baby plant inside the seed.

Big apple trees grow from tiny seeds. This apple has been cut to show one of the seeds inside it.

When the seed begins to grow, it swells up with water. The seed coat breaks open, and a tiny root grows down into the soil. Then the stem and leaves grow upward. The tiny plant is called a seedling.

An Apple Tree Seedling

bud

new leaves

bud

seed leaf

seed leaf (with seed cover)

stem

roots

A bud grows at the end of each branch of an apple tree.

A seedling apple tree has just two leaves.
These leaves are called seed leaves. They
contain food to get the seedling off to a good
start. At the top of the seedling is a bud. A bud
is a place where a new leaf or branch can grow.

These buds are beginning to grow. Buds grow into branches, leaves, or flowers.

The stem of the seedling becomes the trunk of the apple tree. The trunk is strong. It holds up the top of the tree. As the trunk grows, it makes new buds. These buds grow into branches.

New leaves are growing on this young apple tree's branches.

The branches grow and make more branch buds. The young plant begins to look more like a tree. As the little tree grows, leaf buds grow along each branch. Leaves grow from the leaf buds.

New bark is smooth. As an apple tree grows, the outside layer of bark cracks and becomes rough.

The tree's trunk and branches are covered with bark. The hard outside layer of the bark is called cork. It protects the apple tree. The cork is not alive. Just under the cork is the living part of the bark. It carries food from the leaves to the rest of the tree.

While the trunk and branches grow above the ground, the roots grow underground. They hold the tree firmly in the soil. They collect water and minerals from the soil to help the tree grow. The bark carries the water to all parts of the tree.

As a tree grows, its trunk becomes thicker. People have tied this young tree to help it stand up straight.

The apple tree's leaves contain a green substance called chlorophyll (KLOR-uh-fihl). Chlorophyll collects energy from sunlight. Other parts of the leaf collect a gas called carbon dioxide (dy-AHK-side) from the air. The chlorophyll uses water, carbon dioxide, and the sun's energy to make food for the tree. Food helps the plant to grow and make more leaves.

Green leaves make food for an apple tree. The food helps the tree grow apples.

As the summer ends, green apple leaves become brown or yellow.

The apple tree gets bigger every year. Each autumn, its leaves turn brown and yellow. Then the leaves fall off. The tree rests for the winter. In the spring, the tree grows new leaves.

The scientific name of the wild apple tree that grows in Europe and Asia is Malus pumila. *The apple tree people grow is* Malus domestica.

Most of the apple tree's branches grow to be a few feet long. But some branches are different. They stay very short. These special branches are called spurs. Even after growing for many years, a spur is only a few inches long. Spurs produce buds that are less than an inch apart. Some of the spur's buds produce leaves. But others can make flowers.

Apple trees grow many short side branches called spurs. Some of these spurs can produce flowers.

Chapter 3

Apple flowers open in the spring, when the tree is covered with new leaves. How many petals does each apple flower have?

From Flower to Fruit

 Apple trees grow flowers in the spring. This is called blooming. When apple trees bloom, they become covered with pinkish white flowers.

An apple flower has five petals. In the center of the flower are five short, white stalks called styles. Each style has a sticky top. Around the styles are 20 long, thin stalks called stamens (STAY-mehnz). A yellow powder called pollen covers the top of each stamen.

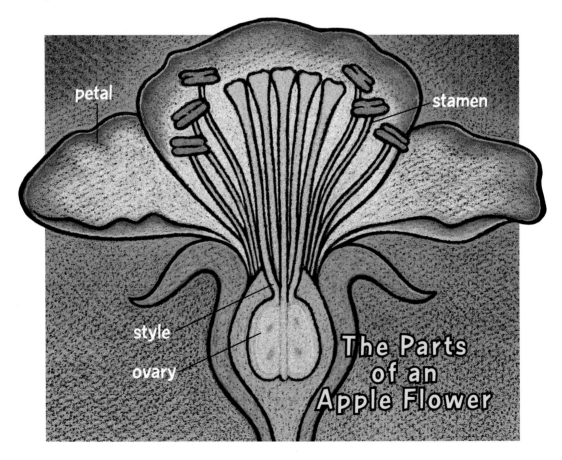

petal

stamen

style

ovary

The Parts of an Apple Flower

An apple tree in bloom buzzes with the sound of hundreds of bees. The bees come to collect food. Bees eat pollen. They also eat nectar, the sweet liquid that flowers make.

These flower buds have just begun to open.

Bees live in these white boxes. The boxes are called beehives. People put beehives near apple trees because bees pollinate apple flowers.

When a bee puts its head in a flower to eat nectar, pollen rubs off the stamens. The pollen sticks to the bee's body. When the bee flies away, it takes the pollen with it. When the bee visits another flower, some pollen may rub off the bee. The pollen may stick to another flower's styles.

There is yellow pollen near the middle of these apple flowers.

Each tiny bit of pollen is called a grain.
When a pollen grain sticks to a flower's style,
a long tube grows out of the grain. The tube

grows down through the style to a part of the flower called the ovary (OH-vuh-ree). When this happens, the flower has been pollinated. For each grain that pollinates the flower, one seed forms.

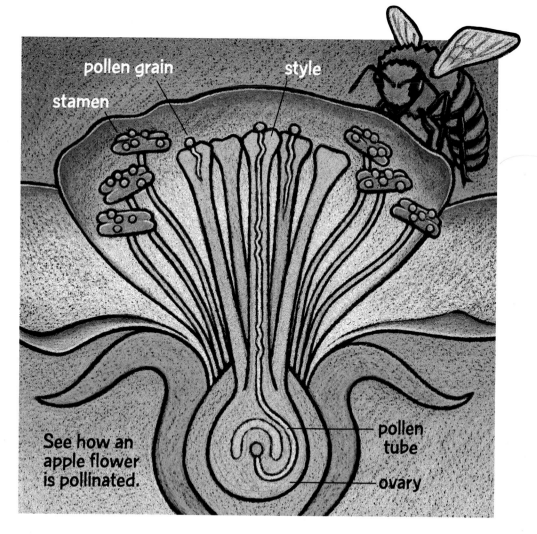

pollen grain

style

stamen

See how an apple flower is pollinated.

pollen tube

ovary

Up to 10 seeds can grow in an apple flower's ovary. Each seed makes auxin (AWK-sihn), a chemical that keeps the ovary from falling off the tree.

Most apple flowers are pink when they open. Some stay pink, but others slowly turn white.

These new apples are just beginning to grow.

A few days after an apple tree blooms, the petals fall to the ground. But the ovaries of pollinated flowers stay on the tree and begin to swell. The swelling ovaries will grow into apples.

Chapter 4

Often many apples grow on the same branch. Why do some of the apples fall off the tree?

Becoming an Apple

As summer begins, the little green apples grow bit by bit. Soon any fruits with fewer than three or four seeds drop off. They don't make enough auxin to stay on the tree.

Often, a tree is crowded with too many apples. Then even more of the young apples fall off.

Many apples fall from apple trees early in the summer. This is called "June drop."

Parts of the apple flower can be seen at the bottom of each of these apples.

During the summer, the fruits get bigger. They look more and more like apples. In the fall, the apples grow more quickly. They start to ripen. The fruits swell up with water and air.

30

Part of the inside of the fruit changes to sweet sugar. These changes happen inside the apple, so they can't be seen.

Many kinds of insects eat apples and apple leaves. Insects made the brown spots on this tree's leaves and fruit.

The outside of the apple changes, too. Red and yellow colors appear in the skin of most kinds of apples. Soon, the apples will be ready to pick and eat.

Some apples turn bright red as they become ripe.

*Some apples turn yellow as they grow. These apples
are almost ready to be picked.*

33

People grow many kinds of apples. How do people grow the kinds of apples they want?

Making an Apple Tree

 There are many varieties (vuh-RYE-uh-teez), or kinds, of apples. Each variety has its own special flavor. People who grow apples want to know what variety of fruit a tree will

produce. But if you plant an apple seed, you can't be sure what the fruit will be like. So apple growers don't grow trees from seeds. Instead, they make the variety of tree they want.

Several different kinds of apple trees are growing in this orchard.

The first step in making an apple tree is to grow a rootstock. The rootstock will form the tree's roots and the bottom of its trunk. Growers choose rootstocks carefully. One rootstock may grow well where winters are cold. Another may grow better where the weather is warmer.

Some rootstocks are made from apple trees. But others are made from crabapple, quince, or pear trees.

*When people make apple trees, they know how tall
the trees will grow to be.*

Some rootstocks produce big trees. Others produce small ones. Full-sized apple trees can be up to 40 feet tall. They may not give much fruit until they are 10 to 20 years old. Smaller trees take up less space. And it's easier to pick apples from small trees. Most apple growers want trees that are 8 to 12 feet tall. These trees start growing fruit after three to five years.

The next step in making a tree is called grafting. The grower chooses a variety of apple to grow. A bud is cut from this variety of apple tree. The bud is attached under the rootstock's bark, and the bud and rootstock grow together.

See how a bud is grafted to a rootstock.

slit in bark

bud

rootstock

The bud is attached under the bark of the rootstock. The bud and the rootstock grow together to become a new apple tree.

The trunk of this young apple tree bends where a bud was attached to the rootstock. The scar shows where the top of the rootstock was cut off.

The trunk and branches of the new tree grow from the grafted bud. So all of the tree's fruit will be the kind the grower wanted.

Chapter 6

This man is picking apples from a tree. What do people make from very small apples?

From Tree to Table

Most apples are easy to pick when they are ripe. People climb ladders to collect the fruit. They put the apples into big wooden bins. The bins are loaded onto trucks and taken to a packing plant.

Each bin contains just one kind of apple. But there are big apples and small ones. There are perfect apples and damaged ones. The apples must be sorted.

First the fruit passes over a wire screen. The smallest apples fall through holes in the screen. These apples are sent to the juice factory.

Only large apples stay on the wire screen. The smallest apples fall through the holes.

At a packing plant, apples float gently in a big tank that is full of water. The water keeps the apples from becoming bruised.

People sort the rest of the apples. They set aside bruised, marked up, or unevenly shaped fruits. These apples don't look nice enough to be sold in grocery stores. They are set aside to be made into applesauce or pies.

Only the best apples are left. They are washed and brushed to clean them. Then they are covered with a special wax to make them shiny. The apples are packed into cardboard boxes. Then they go off to the market so we can all enjoy sweet, crisp apples.

Thousands of different kinds of apples are grown around the world.

On Sharing a Book

As you know, adults greatly influence a child's attitude toward reading. When a child sees you read, or when you share a book with a child, you're sending a message that reading is important. Show the child that reading a book together is important to you. Find a comfortable, quiet place. Turn off the television and limit other distractions, such as telephone calls.

Be prepared to start slowly. Take turns reading parts of this book. Stop and talk about what you're reading. Talk about the photographs. You may find that much of the shared time is spent discussing just a few pages. This discussion time is valuable for both of you, so don't move through the book too quickly. If the child begins to lose interest, stop reading. Continue sharing the book at another time. When you do pick up the book again, be sure to revisit the parts you have already read. Most importantly, enjoy the book!

Be a Vocabulary Detective

You will find a word list on page 5. Words selected for this list are important to the understanding of the topic of this book. Encourage the child to be a word detective and search for the words as you read the book together. Talk about what the words mean and how they are used in the sentence. Do any of these words have more than one meaning? You will find these words defined in a glossary on page 46.

What about Questions?

Use questions to make sure the child understands the information in this book. Here are some suggestions:

> What did this paragraph tell us? What does this picture show? What do you think we'll learn about next? How is an apple tree different from the trees in your backyard? How is it similar? How does an apple tree seedling grow? How do an apple tree's leaves make food for the tree? What are the parts of an apple flower? How do bees help apples grow? Why do some young apples fall off the tree? What is your favorite part of the book? Why?

If the child has questions, don't hesitate to respond with questions of your own, such as: What do *you* think? Why? What is it that you don't know? If the child can't remember certain facts, turn to the index.

Introducing the Index

The index is an important learning tool. It helps readers get information quickly without searching throughout the whole book. Turn to the index on page 47. Choose an entry, such as *flowers,* and ask the child to use the index to find out the time of year when apple trees grow flowers. Repeat this exercise with as many entries as you like. Ask the child to point out the differences between an index and a glossary. (The index helps readers find information quickly, while the glossary tells readers what words mean.)

Where in the World?

Many plants and animals found in the Early Bird Nature Books series live in parts of the world other than the United States. Encourage the child to find the places mentioned in this book on a world map or globe. Take time to talk about climate, terrain, and how you might live in such places.

All the World in Metric!

Although our monetary system is in metric units (based on multiples of 10), the United States is one of the few countries in the world that does not use the metric system of measurement. Here are some conversion activities you and the child can do using a calculator:

WHEN YOU KNOW:	MULTIPLY BY:	TO FIND:
miles	1.609	kilometers
feet	0.3048	meters
inches	2.54	centimeters
gallons	3.787	liters
tons	0.907	metric tons
pounds	0.454	kilograms

Activities

Ask an adult to cut an apple into wedges. Look for seeds in the pieces of apple. An apple can have up to 10 seeds. How many can you find?

Grow your own apple tree. Put some apple seeds in a bowl of water. Soak them in a warm place overnight. The next day, fill some small plastic cups with moist potting soil. Plant a few seeds in each cup, just under the soil's surface. Put the cups in a warm, dark place. Keep the soil moist, but not wet, and wait for seedlings to appear. Be patient—it may take a few weeks for the seeds to sprout. When the seeds have sprouted, move the cups to a sunny place.

Glossary

auxin (AWK-sihn)—a chemical made by apple seeds that keeps apples from falling off the tree

bud—a part of a plant that grows into a leaf, branch, or flower

carbon dioxide (dy-AHK-side)—a gas that plants use to make food

chlorophyll (KLOR-uh-fihl)—the green substance found in a plant that makes food for the plant

grafting—joining parts of two plants to make a new plant

nectar—a sweet liquid that flowers make

ovary (OH-vuh-ree)—the part of a flower in which seeds form

petals—the colored outer parts of a flower

pollen—yellow powder from a flower that is needed to make seeds

pollinated—pollen has been carried from one flower to another so seeds can form

rootstock—the roots and trunk of a tree that are used in grafting

seedling—a young plant that has grown from a seed

spurs—very short side branches

stamens (STAY-mehnz)—long, thin stalks found in an apple flower

styles—the five short, white stalks in the center of an apple flower

Index

Pages listed in **bold** type refer to photographs.

About the Author

Dorothy Hinshaw Patent was born in Minnesota and spent most of her growing-up years in Marin County, California. She has a Ph.D. in zoology from the University of California. She has a special love for apples, as her grandfather owned an apple ranch in Idaho. Dr. Patent is the author of over 90 nonfiction books for children including the titles *Baby Horses, Dogs: The Wolf Within, Horses,* and *Cattle,* published by Carolrhoda Books. Her books have received a number of awards, including the Golden Kite from the Society of Children's Book Writers and Illustrators and the Children's Choice Award from the International Reading Association. She has two grown sons and lives in Missoula, Montana, with her husband, Greg.

About the Photographer

William Muñoz lives with his wife and son in western Montana. He has been photographing nature for over 20 years. Mr. Muñoz exhibits his photographs at art fairs throughout the USA and has collaborated with Dorothy Patent on numerous critically acclaimed books for children.